Mr. Wu's Curiosities

Margaret Su
Illustrated by Aleksey & Olga Ivanov

Rigby®
A Harcourt Achieve Imprint

www.Rigby.com
1-800-531-5015

Chapter One

The Shop of Curiosities

The light tinkle of a bell greeted Sophia as she entered the strange little shop. She hesitated before letting the door swing shut behind her, and then she began to move carefully through the crowded aisles.

The shop was only one small room, and it was stuffed with tables, chairs, cabinets, and shelves, all cluttered with interesting and unusual objects. Cheerful streams of sunlight reached through the front window like glittering fingers, eagerly touching everything within their reach.

For the first time that day, Sophia relaxed, enjoying the feeling that she was walking into a giant treasure chest filled with many marvelous objects.

Wandering a little deeper into the small shop, Sophia let her hand brush across the top of an old chest of drawers, admiring the fancy pattern on its surface. Then she poked at a small stone statue of a fat man perched on a stack of dusty books, and she stooped to look at three wooden ducks on the floor.

As she examined the odd assortment of old furniture and knick-knacks, Sophia wondered where all these abandoned things had come from and who would eventually take these items home.

Then Sophia remembered her purpose and approached the long wooden counter toward the back of the shop. She looked around for the shopkeeper, but when she didn't spot anyone, she finally called out, "Is there anyone here?"

A thick curtain behind the counter was pushed aside, revealing a doorway to a small storage room and an elderly man whose small frame made him not much taller than twelve-year-old Sophia. His face was generously lined with age, and his thick white hair was cut short, as if he had neither the time nor the patience to worry about it.

The man gave Sophia a sharp, questioning look and asked, "Are you here for something?"

What a very odd way to ask if I need help, thought Sophia, *because if I'm here, and I called out, I must be here for something.* However, she just smiled and said, "Yes, I'm looking for a chair that I can use at my desk."

"Well," the man said with a wise nod, "there are certainly many chairs here in this shop."

The old man moved around the counter with surprising speed and headed for the far corner of the room, while Sophia hurried along behind him like a duckling following its mother. Soon they were examining chairs in a variety of sizes, shapes, styles, and conditions.

At last the old man nodded twice, dragged a simple wooden chair from the collection, placed it in front of Sophia, and demanded, "Sit down and let's see if it likes you."

Isn't it a case of whether I like the chair? thought Sophia as she sat carefully on the seat, half-expecting the chair to reject her and dump her on the floor.

After a minute passed with no apparent rejection by the chair, Sophia relaxed, and deciding that it was actually very comfortable, she opened her mouth to say she would like to buy it.

But before Sophia could say the words, the shopkeeper muttered, "Let's see about this," and began walking around her as she sat in the chair. Suddenly he stopped, looked squarely at Sophia, and said, "Yes, you may buy it after all," and whisked the chair out from under her so fast that she almost *did* end up on the floor.

"May I look around for a little while?" Sophia asked when she, the old man, and the chair were back at the counter.

The old man nodded, then ignored Sophia as he turned his attention to a leather-bound book and started to flip through the pages.

Then Sophia noticed a tall china cabinet with glass doors that stood slightly behind the counter and off to one side. Something drew her to it, despite the dark finish, the crack running down one side, and the scratched bronze knobs on the doors.

Overcome with curiosity, Sophia moved forward to look at the strange assortment of objects displayed in the cabinet. The items seemed quite common, but each was displayed on a small square of velvet cloth, while everything else in the shop was piled up here and there on any flat surface with no sign of organization. As Sophia leaned forward and peered through the glass door, she wondered why these things were being treated with such care.

Chapter Two

The Mysterious China Cabinet

Sophia pressed her nose against the cabinet's glass doors as she tried in vain to make sense of the items and why each might have been chosen for such special treatment. Her eyes were drawn to one piece in particular—a miniature version of an old-fashioned well—and she finally turned to the shop owner and asked, "May I please look at that little well in this cabinet?"

The old man glanced up from his book, scanned Sophia's face with bright, curious eyes, nodded, and said, "As long as you understand that these items are not for sale."

Sophia was too timid to ask why a shop would display things that weren't for sale, so she just watched as the old man opened the cabinet door, carefully removed the well, and placed it on the counter for her to see.

Perfect in every detail, the well had a tiny bucket that was attached to a pole by a fine silver thread which was tied to the well's handle. As she imagined the well in the middle of a miniature town square, with miniature people filling miniature buckets with water, Sophia's fingers itched to turn the handle and lower the bucket. She sighed and asked, "Is this part of a special collection of yours?"

The shop owner seemed to be surprised by this, and his face crinkled into a smile as he exclaimed, "No, I do not collect things, for what good would a bunch of things be to me?"

Sophia was puzzled by this answer, but her curiosity was stronger than her shyness, so she tried again, saying, "What I mean is, what are all these things here for, if they're not for sale and you don't collect them?"

The old man shrugged and said, "Well, they are all different, so they are all here for different reasons, and I couldn't say what each is here for without taking all day about it."

Feeling that she was spending an unusual amount of time making herself understood, Sophia tried again and said, "I'm simply wondering why you don't want to sell them."

Clearly surprised by her curiosity, the old man responded by saying, "I did not mean I did not *want* to sell them, but that I *cannot* sell them because I do not own these items."

When Sophia asked who *did* own them, the old man looked at her as if she were speaking a foreign language, shook his head, and said, "Why, they don't belong to anyone; they just turn up here and I let them stay because it keeps them out of trouble."

Sophia opened her mouth to ask another question, found it impossible to come up with anything that made sense, and instead merely said, "Well, my mom is expecting me at home soon, so I'd better pay you for the chair now." The shop owner nodded and carefully placed the miniature well back in its velvet nest on the cabinet shelf.

As Sophia handed over the money, she suddenly remembered her manners and said, "Thank you for letting me look at the little well. It reminds me of a wishing well in my old town that I used to throw pennies into."

The shop owner frowned, knit his brows together thoughtfully, and commented, "Just remember, young lady, that one always needs to be careful what one wishes for, because sometimes wishes that are granted can be problems gained."

Before Sophia could respond to this remark, he handed her a business card that read, "Mr. Wu's Shop of Curiosities."

"Are you Mr. Wu?" she asked.

"I am. And you are?" the old man asked, reaching out and shaking hands with Sophia in a grip that was surprisingly strong.

"I'm Sophia Cruz, and I moved here a few weeks ago with my mother and sister to an apartment a little way down the street, over the coffee shop at the corner of Spaulding Avenue."

"Well then, Sophia Cruz, since we are neighbors, I am sure I will see you in my shop again," said Mr. Wu.

Chapter Three

The Vanity Mirror

Sophia thought about Mr. Wu and his cluttered shop as she walked the three blocks to her apartment. She tried to recall all of the interesting items she had seen there, but her mind kept going back to the miniature well.

Sophia was so intent that she missed her usual landmarks, like the pet shop window where she always stopped to peek in at the kittens. So she was surprised when she realized she had reached the coffee shop.

She walked up the flight of stairs to her home and found her mother and sister already making dinner. "Hey, Mom, I found a chair at Mr. Wu's shop, the one down the street that we passed the other day," she said as she put her things away, then joined them in the kitchen to help set the table.

"I'll pick it up tomorrow after school," Sophia's mother said. Then she added, "How was the rest of your day?"

When Sophia just shrugged, her mother said, "You don't seem very enthusiastic about school, Sophia."

"Well, it's only the second week, Mom, and I don't really know anyone yet, so it's hard to be very excited about things."

"Well," said Mrs. Cruz, "moving means we all have to adjust, and I know you'll do fine and make lots of friends."

Although Sophia knew that this was true, adjusting was something that seemed to come a lot more easily to her mother and sister than it did to her. Sophia's mom was a teacher, and no matter where she worked, she was always one of the most popular teachers in the school. And Maria was, well—Maria, who was smart and pretty and always had a bunch of friends who thought she was the greatest.

And then there's me, thought Sophia, the one member of the family who doesn't seem to be popular, smart, or special in any way.

The family had moved here because Mrs. Cruz had been offered a great teaching position at a new middle school. Sophia attended the school where her mom taught, which was the part of the move that she liked. But it was still a new school, and the hallways were cold and full of strangers who didn't seem to need any more friends.

So here I am, friendless in a strange town with nothing much to do, thought Sophia gloomily.

That night Sophia lay in bed thinking about the little well in Mr. Wu's shop and about what the old man had said about wishes. As long as a person knew exactly what she wanted to wish for, why would she need to be careful about making the wish? Sophia drifted off to sleep considering what she would wish for if she had the opportunity.

The next afternoon, after another day of feeling invisible at school, Sophia found herself pushing open the door to Mr. Wu's shop. As she made her way toward the long wooden counter, Mr. Wu looked up from the huge ornamental mirror he was boxing up and inquired, "Hello, Sophia, what are you looking for today?"

Not wanting to admit that she had only stopped by to look at the things in the cabinet again, Sophia commented, "I've never seen a mirror that big before."

"Well, it's not the size of the mirror that matters, but not being deceived by what one sees in it," said Mr. Wu.

Thinking that Mr. Wu certainly said the most puzzling things, Sophia asked, "How can a mirror deceive you when you see the same thing no matter what mirror you look into?"

Mr. Wu simply raised his eyebrows and commented, "I think it is possible to see things in some mirrors that are not important."

"What you see in any mirror is just a reflection, so how can it be either important or not important?" asked Sophia, wondering if anything about this conversation made sense.

Mr. Wu nodded in satisfaction and said, "Why, you are exactly right, Sophia, because absolutely nothing is important about a person's reflection. If only all mirrors knew that," he concluded with a deep sigh.

Wondering why she even tried to figure out what Mr. Wu meant, Sophia said, "I don't understand—mirrors can't think. So how can a mirror think someone's reflection is important or not?"

Shaking his head as if he had been asked an unanswerable question, Mr. Wu motioned to Sophia to follow him to the china cabinet, where he opened the door and reached for a hand mirror that sat on the bottom shelf. It had an oval frame decorated with flowers and images of tiny fairies.

Holding the mirror out to Sophia, Mr. Wu said, "Now this is a vanity mirror, and it truly lives up to its name. It found its way to me a while ago when its owner asked me to take it in because it had caused her to spend hours gazing at herself and worrying about the color of her hair and the shape of her brows."

Sophia took the mirror carefully from Mr. Wu, thinking that it was even lovelier when viewed up close. The golden metal sparkled in the dim light at the back of the shop, and the fairies seemed ready to fly off the edges.

As she slowly raised the mirror to her face, Sophia noticed that the mirrored glass was clean and crisp. She studied her reflection carefully, realizing that she had never known that her hair was so dark and shiny, or her eyes so big.

At first Sophia admired herself, thinking that the mirrors at home were smudged and dirty and never gave her a true picture of herself, but then she began to notice troubling details. Why had she never seen before that her eyes were such an odd shade of brown, and had her nose always had that strange little crook at the end?

When Mr. Wu gently took the mirror from her hand, Sophia jumped, then nearly snatched it back, wanting to get a closer look at her left ear to see if its curve exactly matched the curve of her right ear.

Mr. Wu sighed and asked, "Now do you see why I say this mirror is such a silly and wasteful thing, Sophia?"

"But it's not silly, Mr. Wu; it's absolutely wonderful," cried Sophia. "Why, this is the first time I have ever seen myself so clearly!"

Mr. Wu shook his head and calmly said, "Oh, Sophia, even the best mirrors cannot show clearly who you are, no matter how long you spend with them. Do you realize that you have been gazing into this one for 30 minutes?"

Sophia gasped and looked at the clock on the counter, wondering how she could have spent so long looking in a mirror, and why the time had seemed so short.

As Mr. Wu placed the mirror back in the cabinet, he said, "There is so much more to people than what we can see, Sophia, that it is foolish to spend too much time worrying about an image in a mirror."

Sophia was hardly listening because a strange idea had suddenly occurred to her, and now she blurted out, "Mr. Wu, is that mirror—and everything else in the cabinet—magical?"

"Let's not give these things any magical properties, Sophia, for they are just what they are and always have been," said Mr. Wu.

Sophia realized this was the only answer she would get from the puzzling Mr. Wu, so she swallowed the rest of the questions that bubbled up inside her.

The bell at the door sounded as a tall, thin man entered the shop. Rubbing his hands together happily, Mr. Wu moved to the front of the shop to greet his customer.

While Mr. Wu was occupied, Sophia went back to the china cabinet and peered through the glass doors, wondering about the stories behind the other items on the shelves.

Chapter Four

The Wishing Well

None of the objects in the china cabinet look that unusual, Sophia thought, *especially the copper penny sitting on top of one piece of velvet.* Thinking that pennies were everywhere and that this one seemed perfectly ordinary, Sophia looked away to gaze again at the strangely fascinating miniature well.

When the bell signaled the departure of the tall, thin man, and Mr. Wu walked back to the counter, Sophia asked, "May I look at the little well again?"

Mr. Wu opened the cabinet, pulled out the well, placed it in front of Sophia, and said, "Since you find this so interesting, I suppose that you may as well try it out."

Sophia took a deep breath, reached out to turn the tiny handle, and watched the silver rope unwind as the tiny wooden bucket disappeared into the well.

"We used to live near a plaza that had a fountain shaped like a wishing well," she said as if talking to herself. "My sister and I would have so much fun as we tossed coins into the water and made our wishes."

Mr. Wu nodded his head as if he truly understood her sadness and loneliness, then commented, "A well is a natural place for making wishes, especially a well that is filled with water to throw coins into." He pointed to the miniature well on the counter and said, "This well, though now dry, has certainly seen more than its share of wishes."

"It *is* a wishing well, isn't it?" cried Sophia, her eyes dancing. "Please, can I make a wish, Mr. Wu?" she begged, clasping her hands and looking hopeful.

The old man gazed at Sophia with concern for a moment before protesting, "A wishing well is a very serious matter, and I was not suggesting you do anything so rash as to wish with this one. Haven't you heard the saying, 'Be careful what you wish for, for it just may come true'?"

Sophia shook her head, laughed, and said, "No, and anyway, I can't imagine why you would make a wish if you didn't want it to come true."

The thought of making a wish—even a tiny one—made Sophia feel happier than she had felt in weeks. First, however, the well needed water, so she gathered up her nerve and asked, "May I put a little bit of water in the well before I make a wish?"

Mr. Wu hesitated, then said, "Sophia, I can tell you are not taking the business of wishing seriously, so I must warn you that this well has already caused a bit of mischief to those who have used it."

Not ready to give up, Sophia said, "Mr. Wu, I'm not worried, because my life can't get much worse than it already is—living in a new town where I don't know anyone and I don't have one single friend."

Mr. Wu was quiet for a moment, but at last he sighed and said, "I can see it is no use arguing with you, so I will get you your water." He disappeared into the curtained space behind the counter and returned a minute later with a small glass of water and a tiny spoon.

Sophia put a few drops of water into the bucket, and then, with great ceremony, she lowered it into the well.

As soon as the bucket hit the bottom of the well, Sophia squeezed her eyes shut and made her wish. Then she turned the handle and raised the bucket, discovering that it was now empty and dry.

Sophia peered into the little wishing well and was surprised when she didn't see any sign that the water had spilled. She looked up at Mr. Wu and said, "Where in the world did the water go?"

Mr. Wu's expression gave no sign of his earlier concern, but instead his eyes now sparkled with laughter as he replied, "Well, wishing wells will want water! Ha—try saying that five times!"

They both tried to repeat the phrase, and ended up tongue-tied and giggling so hard that they cried.

At last Mr. Wu wiped the tears from his eyes and stated, "My, my, I haven't laughed this hard in a very long time."

Sophia, who had finally stopped giggling herself, glanced at the clock and exclaimed, "Oh, it's later than I thought, so I'd better head home before Mom starts to worry."

As Mr. Wu waved her to the door, he called out, "I hope to see you again, Sophia, as you surely do brighten up my day."

During dinner, Sophia toyed with her food while her mind wandered back to the well and how strange it was that the water had disappeared when she made her wish.

"Sophia, why are you so quiet?" Maria asked, interrupting Sophia's thoughts.

Sophia glanced up, and her eyes went from her sister's concerned face to her mother's equally concerned one. "What would you wish for if you could have one wish?" she blurted.

"Why in the world are you thinking about wishes, Sophia?" her mother asked.

"Just for the fun of it, Mom," Sophia reassured her.

Mrs. Cruz smiled and said, "Well, in that case, I'd wish that you girls would pick up your things and help me clean more often."

"Oh, Mom," said Sophia, "how about wishing for a big castle and a stable full of horses or something else that's fun?"

But Mrs. Cruz shook her head and insisted that castles and stables were just too hard to keep clean.

Then Maria said seriously, "Well, I've thought about it and decided that my wish is for everyone in the world to have enough to eat."

Trust Maria to wish for something good and wonderful and unselfish, thought Sophia. "What about wishing for something just for you—like new friends?" she asked her sister.

Maria shook her head and said, "But that's something you can do for yourself, Sophia, so why would you waste a wish on it?"

Sophia shrugged and said softly, "I guess because it's what I'd really like to have happen, that's why."

Her mother smiled as she explained, "Sophia, friendship is something you work on, not something you wish for."

Maybe it works like that for you and Maria, thought Sophia, *but it's harder for someone like me, and wishing can't hurt.*

Then she smiled because the doubts of her mother and sister didn't really matter. After all, she had already made her wish, and now, with the help of Mr. Wu's wishing well, she was almost sure that it would come true.

Chapter Five

Do Wishes Come True?

The next morning, Sophia found herself thinking about the well as she entered the science room. The day stretched out before her endlessly, but the thought of stopping by the shop on the way home cheered her up.

The teacher, Mr. Harrison, interrupted Sophia's thoughts by saying, "Sophia, I was talking to your mother in the teacher's room before school and she had some great things to say about you."

Taken aback, Sophia could only respond, "She did?"

"Yes, she said that your curiosity makes you a wonderful researcher. She also told me about the sea life project you worked on, and she said that you won several awards at your other school."

Sophia frowned, thinking that her mother must have been talking about Maria and Mr. Harrison had just gotten the name wrong.

As he continued speaking, Mr. Harrison shuffled through a stack of papers on his desk, so he missed the expression on Sophia's face. "You know the class will be breaking into groups for projects, and we'll be looking at topics that need a lot of careful research," he said.

Then the teacher raised his head, gave Sophia a big smile, and said, "I imagine you'll find yourself in demand because any group will be happy to have an experienced researcher as part of the team."

"Oh, yeah, I guess," mumbled Sophia, struggling to think of a way to straighten out this misunderstanding before it got even worse than it already was. However, before she could say anything, the bell rang and she had to take her usual seat in front of Ankur.

Most days Ankur barely looked at Sophia, but today he went to her and said, "Hey, I heard what Mr. Harrison said about all your awards and about doing research at sea, too."

Then another girl asked, "Where have you done all this traveling?"

Next Peter called out, "You must be pretty smart to win an award."

By now other students were listening, and Sophia could feel her face growing red as she tried to figure out how to put an end to this misunderstanding. But before she could say anything, Ankur tapped her on the shoulder and announced that he hoped she'd be in his group, and Peter protested that he wanted Sophia in *his* group.

Sophia was confused by all this sudden attention, until she remembered the wishing well and wondered if her wish for friends and popularity was actually coming true.

Then Mr. Harrison called his students to attention and explained that they would work in groups to come up with ideas for projects that fit the theme "How Things Work." When the teacher was done assigning groups, Sophia found herself teamed up with Ankur, Peter, and a quiet girl named Monique.

As soon as the group sat down together, Ankur started talking, with Peter interrupting often. Unfortunately, as far as Sophia could tell, the biggest contribution made by either boy was to name topics they *didn't* want to work on, and to talk so much that she and Monique didn't have a chance to say anything.

When Ankur and Peter finally paused for a breath, Monique turned to Sophia and said, "You must have an idea, Sophia."

Sophia stared at Monique, and her mind went completely blank until she heard Ankur ask impatiently, "Well?"

Suddenly words started swirling in Sophia's head: well, wishes, wishing well, water . . . She looked at the others, and then said the last word that had come to mind, "Water."

As the other three stared at her in confusion, inspiration finally hit Sophia and the words spilled out as she explained, "Yes, water—like where does it come from and where does it go?"

Ankur snorted and said, "It comes from the sky, of course, and then it goes down the drain."

Sophia ignored him, excited by her idea as she continued, "We could investigate water reservoirs and the disposal of wastewater."

Monique smiled and said, "I think that idea has a lot of possibilities, like water conservation and filtration systems."

Ankur shrugged and said, "It sounds like you have a great idea and know what to do with it."

Peter went on to say, "We're supposed to have an outline done by Monday, so why don't you work on that, Sophia, since it should be a snap for someone with your research skills? You can be our group leader, and we'll all work on the report once you figure out what we need to do."

"Group leader," Sophia repeated, nodding her head as she decided that she actually liked the sound of that.

Later, while Sophia was gathering up her books at the end of class, Ankur came up and said, "Hey, Peter and I are going for some ice cream after school and wondered if you'd like to come."

Sophia was going to say yes when Peter added, "Yeah, we want to hear about the places you've been."

"Sorry, guys," said Sophia, "but I can't make it today."

Chapter Six

The Lucky Penny

The bell on the shop door rang sharply as Sophia hurried in early Saturday morning, rushed to the counter, and hopped from foot to foot while Mr. Wu finished with a customer. At last the old man turned to her, pulled a stool out from behind the counter, and said, "Goodness gracious, Sophia, settle down and sit here."

As soon as Sophia was perched on the stool, Mr. Wu smiled and said, "All right, Sophia, now tell me what in the world has you so excited this Saturday morning."

"Mr. Wu, the wishing well worked!" Sophia exclaimed, hardly able to sit still while she told the story. "I mean, I know I asked if it was magical, but I never really thought it was, until I realized that it actually worked, so it *must* be magical! I got to school yesterday and suddenly I had friends—just like I'd wished—if only—"

When Mr. Wu looked at her with a question in his eyes, Sophia continued, "If only it wasn't all a lie and I wasn't going to be friendless again when they find out."

At Mr. Wu's urging, Sophia described her teacher's misunderstanding and how it had become such a big deal. "So now everyone thinks I'm a brainy world traveler with lots of research experience," she moaned as she told Mr. Wu how she had ended up with the responsibility of doing an outline on a topic she knew nothing about.

"Well," said Mr. Wu, "I am sure everything will be fine once you explain things to your new friends."

"I'm not so sure about that, and it's all my fault anyway, because I should never have made that stupid wish!"

Mr. Wu patted her hand and said, "Now, Sophia, wishes are just puffs of wind and flights of fancy, so do not worry and do not take them too seriously."

"That's not what you said yesterday!" wailed Sophia as she put her head in her hands. "You warned me to be careful what I wished for, but I didn't listen, and look what happened!"

"Oh, child, life would be boring without a bit of difficulty, although there *is* one thing that concerns me about your story," Mr. Wu said.

Sophia raised her eyes to his and asked, "What's that?"

"You say the others in your group have asked you to do all the work?"

Trying to explain, Sophia said, "The guys just think I'm the best one for the job because I'm supposedly good at research."

Mr. Wu shook his head and retorted, "Sophia, it sounds like they are using your skills as a way to get out of work themselves."

"I'm sure you're wrong, since they're meeting me at the library later today."

Sophia paused, recalling the conversation in class, then admitted, "Well, Monique said she would meet me, but I guess Ankur and Peter are waiting to see what I come up with first."

Mr. Wu continued to look disapproving as he softly said, "I think you have a problem because your friends are taking advantage of you, Sophia."

"Mr. Wu, the real problem is that I don't know anything about all this water stuff, and

I don't have a clue how to start the outline," complained Sophia.

When Mr. Wu suggested that Sophia just needed to put some thought into the matter, she muttered, "No, what I need is a lot of luck."

"Oh, Sophia," said Mr. Wu, "luck is an unreliable friend, which is why I offer this advice: work hard enough and you will get what you want without having to depend on luck."

While Mr. Wu went to help a customer, Sophia thought about her new friends and wondered how their feelings would change when they found out she wasn't as fascinating as they thought.

Then she started thinking about the outline she was supposed to do and that worried her even more. If she could do a great job, at least

part of her problem would be solved, but she had no idea how to pull that off.

Sophia's gaze rested for a moment on Mr. Wu's cabinet of mysterious items, thinking that if the wishing well had worked, maybe something else in the cabinet might be helpful.

As she moved forward, Sophia spotted something gleaming on the floor, bent down, and picked up a penny. Although the coin was so worn with age that the date was barely readable, it seemed to shine with an inner light, and she couldn't help murmuring, "I wonder . . . "

Sophia peered into the cabinet, trying to remember where she had seen a penny. There, on the middle shelf, was a faded outline where the penny had once sat on a piece of velvet.

"Mr. Wu!" she exclaimed when he returned, "I think this penny fell out of the cabinet."

Mr. Wu just sighed and said, "Oh, yes, it does like to show off." Then he waved Sophia away when she tried to hand him the penny and told her, "Keep it for now, and return it when you are done."

When Sophia looked confused, Mr. Wu raised his eyebrows and said, "Well, it is a penny, is it not?"

Sophia turned the seemingly normal copper penny over in her hand, wondering if she was understanding Mr. Wu correctly.

"I bet it's a lucky penny, isn't it—like in the old saying, 'Find a penny, pick it up, and all day long you'll have good luck.'"

"Hmmm . . . I may have heard that saying," admitted Mr. Wu, going on to tell Sophia that she should concentrate on making her own luck and not depend on luck to come to her just because she had found a penny.

When the old man stopped talking, Sophia grinned and said, "Well, you did say I could have the penny for a while, Mr. Wu, so maybe I really won't need to make my own good luck after all."

Mr. Wu shook his head and commented, "'Maybes' are fine, but what I know for sure is that if you work hard on your project, everything will turn out fine."

"Maybe," said Sophia with a laugh, as she tucked the lucky penny in her pocket for safekeeping and waved good-bye.

Chapter Seven

Luck and Ice Cream

At the library, Sophia found a good spot near a window, spread out her papers and note cards, and sat back to wait for luck to come her way. However, she began to feel restless as the minutes slowly crawled by and nothing happened. She shifted in her chair, rearranged her things, and finally decided to get up and move around. After all, she thought, the penny is in my pocket, so I don't need to sit in one place.

As Sophia walked up and down the aisles, she glanced casually at the books, thinking that Mr. Wu might be right, and she might actually have to do some reading and work on the outline. Then she saw a shelf labeled *Natural Science* and whispered, "Now, this looks promising."

Suddenly Sophia tripped over a book on the floor and grabbed hold of the nearest shelf to steady herself. Right before her eyes was a large, blue book with the title *Water and How It Works*.

Sophia erupted in laughter, then clapped a hand over her mouth before the librarian could shush her. "It *is* my lucky day," she whispered as she noticed that almost every book on the

shelf had a title that had something to do with water.

Sophia gathered a stack big of books and hurried back to her table. She now had all the information she could possibly need, but she still had to read through it and produce an outline. She was working intently when a tap on the shoulder startled her.

"Sorry," Monique whispered, "but I thought you might want some help, even if you are awfully good at this."

Sophia grinned, admitted that help would be welcome, and then explained what she had been doing while Monique listened.

The next hour zipped past, and doing research had never seemed like such fun. To Sophia, it seemed as if the books fell open to just the pages they needed and great ideas came quickly and easily.

Checking to be sure that the penny was still in her pocket, Sophia thought about what Mr. Wu had said and decided that no matter what, a bit of luck was nice to have.

Shortly after noon, Monique yawned, stretched, and suggested that they meet again after lunch to finish up. The girls parted at the library door and Sophia headed home, feeling grateful that Monique was willing to come back to help.

After a quick lunch, Sophia was headed back to the library when she rounded the corner and ran right into Ankur and Peter. When she told the boys where she was headed, they suggested that she come with them instead, to the best ice cream place in town.

"You have to admit that eating ice cream sounds like more fun than going to the library, Sophia," laughed Peter.

Sophia was thinking that perhaps this was part of her lucky streak, and that it wasn't a good idea to say no to an invitation from her new friends, when she suddenly remembered Monique.

"I really shouldn't," she said slowly, "because Monique will be at the library working on our project, and I told her I'd be there, too."

"I wouldn't worry about it," insisted Ankur, "because you've probably done most of the work already."

When Sophia protested that there was still a lot to do before Monday, Ankur and Peter told her ice cream would make them thirsty, and then they could all think about water and how it works.

Sophia laughed at that, thinking that she *did* deserve a treat because she *had* done a lot of work, and it wouldn't take Monique long to finish.

Once they reached the ice cream shop, things just seemed to get better and better. They got to sit at the best table, right in the sunny window; Sophia's favorite flavor was on special; Peter and Ankur were full of compliments about her ideas for the project; and they laughed when she told a joke.

All the way home Sophia held the lucky penny tightly in one hand, thinking that it had certainly done its job.

Chapter Eight

The Frog Charm

On Sunday afternoon, Sophia stopped by Mr. Wu's shop to return the penny and found him at the counter, removing a small, square jeweler's box from a cardboard carton. Inside, resting on black velvet, Sophia saw a silver charm shaped like a frog with a delicate crown on its head.

Mr. Wu glanced up from the jewelry box, accepted the coin from her, and said, "Ah, yes, how was your day with the penny?"

So Sophia told him all about her day: how she had found the information she had needed, Monique had showed up to help, she had gone for ice cream with friends, and they had really seemed to like her.

"Oh, Mr. Wu, the lucky penny really worked, and that's why it was such a wonderful day!" Sophia summed up.

Mr. Wu studied her for a moment before asking thoughtfully, "And did Monique join you and the others for this ice cream party?"

When Sophia shook her head, the old man said, "I suppose that it *is* lucky that Monique was so willing to do the group's work on her own—at least it was lucky for you."

Sophia felt a tingle of guilt as she explained, "It was mostly done, Mr. Wu, so it probably didn't take her very long to finish . . . at least I don't think it did."

Mr. Wu just nodded and said, "Well, then, I am glad everything worked out nicely for you."

Sophia sensed that Mr. Wu didn't really approve, but he of all people should understand that everything that had happened was due to the wishing well and the lucky penny, and not to anything she had done—right or wrong!

Mr. Wu pulled a card out of the cardboard carton, studied it for a moment, and then read it aloud. "Mr. Wu, please take care of this charm because I am tired of being charming all the time, and I now know that sometimes it's better to just be a frog."

Sophia wondered what that was supposed to mean, but just watched silently as Mr. Wu picked up the silver frog and let it dangle from his fingers, the crown sparkling in the sunlight. Finally her curiosity got the better of her, and she inquired, "Well, what does the charm do?"

When Mr. Wu snorted and said that the charm most likely did something silly, Sophia gathered up her courage and asked, "May I borrow it for a while?"

Mr. Wu stared at Sophia's eager face for a long moment before saying, "Certainly," placing the charm in its box, and pushing both across the counter. "Just remember, Sophia," he warned, "that sometimes learning to be yourself is more worthwhile than trying to be something you are not."

"I'm sure you're right," Sophia replied, "but it's a charm, Mr. Wu, and maybe it will make me 'charming,' which would be a big help," she added with a laugh.

Mr. Wu shook his head and said, "No, Sophia, you do not need help in that area, and besides, I have found that too much charm can be a tiresome thing."

As she walked home with the small box tucked safely into her pocket, Sophia wondered how someone could have too much charm—she was sure that charm was all she needed to complete the process of making new friends.

Chapter Nine

Charm School

When Sophia entered science class with the frog charm dangling merrily from her backpack, Monique walked up to her and handed her the finished outline without responding to Sophia's, "Hi, Monique!"

After Sophia had presented her group's outline, Mr. Harrison praised the work, telling Sophia that he was sure the entire group appreciated her contributions and that he looked forward to an excellent report. The more he said, the more guilty Sophia felt, but the teacher moved on to another group before she could explain that Monique had actually done more than she had.

Peter and Ankur, on the other hand, seemed to have no problem taking credit for work they hadn't done. And when Ankur said something about being a great team, Sophia surprised herself by saying, "Yeah, the Ice Cream Team."

Ankur and Peter burst into laughter, but Monique just looked confused.

For the rest of the day, Sophia was exceptionally clever and witty, and always seemed to know just what to say to make her classmates laugh.

The next day, during lunch, a tall, skinny boy slipped on a piece of lettuce and Sophia quipped, "That slimy salad certainly seems slippery." Someone at her table repeated the phrase, and soon everyone—except the boy who had slipped—was laughing and saying the words as fast as possible.

By the end of the week, however, Sophia couldn't help but realize that some kids were avoiding her. Then, when a boy dropped his history assignment, scattering papers all over the floor, and Sophia said, "Well, *that* report is history!" she got a few nasty looks and almost

no one laughed. After that, she bent her head over her book and didn't say another word for the rest of the class.

On Friday afternoon, as Sophia pushed open the door to Mr. Wu's shop, the familiar sound of the bell seemed less welcoming than usual. She walked to the back where Mr. Wu was sitting at the counter having a cup of tea. He took one look and said, "Sit down, Sophia, and tell me why you appear so troubled."

Sophia settled onto a stool, placed the boxed charm on the counter, and said, "Mr. Wu, I thought I had gotten my wish because I wished for friends, and it seemed like I got some. Then I thought the charm would help me be funny and that would make them like me even more, but instead I ended up not even liking myself very much."

Speaking in solemn tones, Mr. Wu said, "Sophia, if you try to discover who you are, not who you wish to be, I think you may like what you find."

Sophia nodded, then rose from the stool and quietly left the shop.

At home that evening, as Sophia helped her mother make dinner, Mrs. Cruz said,

"Mr. Harrison tells me you're an excellent project leader."

Guilt quickly surged through Sophia as she remembered that she hadn't done a thing about the report in days, despite the fact that she was supposed to be the group leader.

"He only *thinks* I'm doing a good job," she said, keeping her eyes on the salad she was fixing, "and that's because you said something to him about Maria being a great researcher and winning awards and he thought you meant me."

When Mrs. Cruz said, "I *did* mean you," Sophia slowly raised her eyes to look at her mother's face.

"You *are* smart, Sophia, and you are a great researcher. Don't you remember how much you helped Maria with the report she did last year—and what about the prizes you got for your speeches at your old school?"

Sophia shook her head and muttered, "Those were no big deal—not like all the awards Maria gets."

"Sophia," scolded Mrs. Cruz, "you are forgetting that your sister is four years older than you are, so of course she has accomplished things that you haven't. But you know how proud of you I am, so why would you assume I was talking about Maria?"

Sophia tried to wrap her mind around the knowledge that her mother had been talking about her after all, so Mr. Harrison's praise had been real, not a mistake. The mistakes were mine, she thought, and I've made plenty of them.

All through dinner, Sophia's mind raced, thinking about the fact that she had been afraid that people wouldn't like her for herself, and all that had happened was that she had ended up not liking herself. She decided it was time to go back to being the old Sophia.

Chapter Ten

Finding Friends

After school on Monday, Sophia approached Ankur and Peter, and said, "Hey, guys, let's work on our project after school today."

To her surprise, the boys looked first at her and then at each other before Peter said, "Well, we just figured you were taking care of it, since you're so good at this kind of thing and it's easy for you."

"Yeah, and besides, we're both pretty busy this afternoon," added Ankur, going on to say that they didn't know anything about the topic anyway, especially since Sophia had done all the research and the outline.

As the two boys walked off, shoving each other and laughing, Sophia came to the sad realization that they had never really been her friends—they had just wanted her to do their work for them.

Suddenly Sophia recalled her mother's words: friendship was something you worked on, not wished for. She had spent too much time wishing and too little time working, but hopefully, there was time to fix that problem.

After school, Sophia headed for the library where she discovered Monique busily writing at the table near the window, a huge pile of books stacked beside her.

As Sophia approached, Monique looked up in surprise, then smiled and exclaimed, "Hey, Sophia, I sure hope you're going to tell me you're here to help finish this report, because I need you!"

Still feeling guilty, Sophia returned the smile and said, "Well, it *is* supposed to be a group project, and since I think the group has turned out to be just the two of us, I figured I'd better do my part."

"That's good enough for me," said Monique.

For the next two days, the girls worked on their project every chance they got. Sophia discovered that she was actually pretty good at research, even without the lucky penny, and that her friendship with Monique was growing, even without the frog charm. For one thing, both girls had the same slightly wacky sense of humor, so when Monique read aloud from one book, "Walter Windom went whale watching," Sophia just had to repeat the sentence several times. Soon they were both giggling so hard that the librarian had to shush them with a stern look.

At last the report was done, and the girls were headed to Sophia's house to celebrate with ice cream.

On Saturday afternoon, Sophia stopped at Mr. Wu's shop and found him on a ladder, placing a broom on the top of the china cabinet. When she asked what he would do when he needed the broom, Mr. Wu replied, "This broom is only good for sweeping one's troubles away, and that is something a person should do for himself."

Then, descending the ladder and rubbing his dusty hands together, Mr. Wu asked, "So, Sophia, are your troubles taken care of?"

Laughing slightly, Sophia said, "Well, Mr. Harrison said Monique and I had done a great job, but Ankur and Peter didn't fool him a bit. Now they have to write a report on their own—about how to do research."

"So it seems that you have found a friend at your new school?"

A broad smile stretched across Sophia's face as she replied, "Yes, Mr. Wu, I believe I have— one good friend at school, and one here, too."